The Ultimate Guide To Healing Your Past

Learn To Heal Your Past

Through Stories And Exercises

Copyright 2015 by Frank Healy

Frank Healy

To all of my former teachers, current friends, family, and everyone whom I have learned from, Thank you for all of the wonderful life lessons and great memories.

Contents

Frank Healy

Preface

After I published "Heal Your Memories, Change Your Life" It soared to several bestseller lists, including bestsellers for memory, healing, happiness, and cognitive neuroscience. Many people connected with me on Twitter and my Facebook page, Frank Healy, Author.

With this many people interested in my work, I began thinking that there could be another use for your memories besides healing the feelings. It occurred to me that some people never read a book once they complete their formal schooling. Of course, you are not in that category if you are reading this and have finished school. If you are a student, keep learning throughout your life.

For my own part, despite my master's degree and my memory of every day for almost the past 50 years, I am always aware that I have a lot to learn. There is the old adage "Learn something every day". From that idea came the thought that many of us miss opportunities to learn. People can learn from their past and it does not matter if you did not learn the lesson from an incident when it happened. You can learn it now.

You have a large treasure chest of lessons embedded in your memories. The key to learning more about you, life, and success is to learn from everything that has happened. Learning from events that happened long ago can enrich your life and make you wise and successful.

Frank Healy

Reading "The Ultimate Guide To Healing Your Past" will take you through a variety of techniques to help you learn from all of your memories. As a Licensed Professional Counselor and Life Coach, I have used these techniques to help countless clients.

If you read "Heal Your Memories, Change Your Life" you know how you can heal the feelings from past memories, and you know how to access more happy memories. Now you will learn how to extract valuable lessons from those memories. This will help you advance in life as you have more knowledge. When you have learned to learn from your memories you can apply the knowledge to immediately learn from anything that happens in the present.

Each of us would like to consider ourselves intelligent and believe we know how to navigate the journey of life we are on. We want our relationships to work, to fare well on our jobs and like them, and to know how to handle situations. The Ultimate Guide To Healing Your Past will help you mine the treasures of your memories by teaching you to learn from everything.

Introduction

If we were to draw a diagram of Frank Healy's brain, the rendering would most assuredly resemble a file cabinet. How else could Frank categorize his abundant life experiences because unlike you and me, he happens to remember details from every day of his life beginning around the age of five. By placing his memories into useful folders, he catalogues the enigmas of life into precious clusters, all set for him to squeeze out his valuable insights, which he generously shares with us. He graciously offers his stored personal memories and tells us what he learned from those. We glean by example how to benefit from our own past occurrences that most often merely dance around us and collapse into a heap from which we are too overcome to emerge.

Thank you, Frank Healy, from those of us who don't have your "phenomenal memory". As you've observed from those around you and from your counseling and coaching practice, the rest of us live in a dreamlike memory vault with our distortions adhering loyally to each thought. And how do we make use of all these stored up early life treasures? How do we enhance our emotional well-being? Even when we are convinced that we remember the "accurate" details and we act on these make-believe tales in our *real* life, invariably we get into emotional trouble!

So, it's confusing enough that we think we know the facts, but in reality, we store our fairy tales all over the place and as we get snowed under, we pry them out for further dysfunctional filtering.

In his books, Frank Healy comes to the rescue. By opening his brain for our perusal, he teaches us that there are effective ways to hoard and subsequently make use of our experiences. Wow. We are overwhelmed. But then Frank helps us to unlatch the drawer and thumb through our *own* categories. We extract the good stuff along with photos of the rough stuff and hopefully, we learn. Oh, do we learn. Thank you, Frank Healy.

It's been said that smart people have trouble teaching others because they can't lower themselves to their student's level, get inside his or her head to "see" how the other guy's brain actually functions. These genius teachers are just too smart and have never struggled valiantly for knowledge. Frank has embraced his gems and watered them down for the rest of us.

Frank grew up with a gift that some might have seen as a liability. Through his wisdom and persistence, he adapted that trait for the rest of us simple folk. By way of example, he offers us his vulnerability; he invites us into the core of his psyche, one that he has researched and for which he has applied his own teachings.

Frank gently urges us to practice cognitive skills, but then he also nurtures us through the painstaking process: "If you didn't learn something at the time the memory actually happened, perhaps it just wasn't the right time to do so, or perhaps you were too young to really think about the event in a logical way. You don't need to be concerned if the right memory surfaces, nor if you need to heal every one. The right memories will surface at the right times."

The Ultimate Guide To Healing Your Past

He shows us how to view ourselves and our memories from a distance with a new and refreshing slant. We learn why we must not allow our suffering to debilitate us as we become a participant in our own change process. And through this activity, we get to shed some of our anxiety, tension, and pain. Very cool. It's as if we are tricking ourselves to believe that maybe we are not so anxious after all, but we are merely doing a research project!

How we formerly dealt with our pain and how we got through it assures us that we can master our destiny as it rides again! Through Frank's examples, we understand that we are hardy. Even extremely traumatic, uncontrollable, no-fault memories and the commensurate survival mechanisms we crafted in the past helped equip us to face today's new challenges.

Frank relates various stories of heartbreak and resolution, of failure and success as his real life characters adapt, look back, look forward and use their memories to guide them to greater heights. These heroes might have gotten stuck when they fell, or allowed their abusive past to color their lives forever but they stayed the course and maximized their outcomes. Frank uses their personal histories to illustrate his lessons and we are given hope that we, too, might be able to rise above our situation.

Mr. Healy presents his pearls and we learn and we learn and we learn: "The brain tries to solve current problems by reminding you of similar scenarios in the past. The specific memories that the brain recalls in these situations are the ones you need to heal and learn."

Through his wisdom, persistence and handholding, our illustrious teacher encourages us to absorb value from our positive memories as well as the ones that plague us. He gently hammers through his core advice: "rah.rah. rah. Feel the pain

Frank Healy

of your memories, heal them, learn from them, and you will move towards a more fulfilling life."

Phyliss Merion Shanken
Psychologist & Author

Conversations with Perfect Strangers: Memoirs of a
Psychologist
pshanken.com
Co-Founder of lionsoup.com

Chapter 1

We All Have Good Days And Bad Days...Or Do We?

He remembered everything. Good days, bad days, mixed days. It was all catalogued in his brain. Just like computers have folders and files, he had mental folders that catalogued good and bad events. If you were to name a day of the year, he would go through a folder in his brain for every year and tell you what day of the week it was, whether it was raining or the sun was shining, news stories around the world, and personal events. Additionally, he could tell you which folder each day was in: Fun to Remember, Pain in the Brain, or Mixed Bag.

In the folder called Fun to Remember, he stored memories of many good times at the beach, winning awards in school and contests, crawling through man holes with his friends and feeling grateful to have survived afterwards. He also had memories of fun times with girlfriends, hysterical bursts of laughter at Thanksgiving dinners, vacations with his grandparents, going to the fair across the street on his birthday as a child, being in shows such as his ninth grade play where he was the gardener at a college and he didn't know that the other students were witches. The play made for some hilarious lines.

Fun to Remember also includes his few and far between athletic feats such as on Saturday, June 19, 1971, when he made two catches in baseball that saved the game. There are the memories of swimming a couple of miles in the Olympic sized pool at college.

He would take the fraternity brothers to swim with him so they would get in shape after all the beer they drank. There are also good times on vacation with the family in this folder, including the time on Thursday, August 4, 1966, when they went out in the bay on a row boat and dropped the oar.

But then there is also the Pain in the Brain folder. It includes the time on Thursday, July 31, 1975, when he was taunted by a bigger kid who looked like a walrus on the beach. Wow, at least he fared better then mob leader Jimmy Hoffa who disappeared that same day. On Tuesday, May 11, 1976, a man on a bulldozer with a foul mouth chased he and his friend out of a construction site. There was a lot of caroling on Christmas Eve, 1974, a Tuesday when his father dropped a television on his own toe. Another painful event was on Monday, December 15, 1975, when he didn't get the part in the production of *The Music Man* that he practiced and tried out for.

Then there were times in sports, too many to mention, when he struck out or bobbled the ball in baseball. Then there was Friday, March 30, 1979, when he had to pledge to his fraternity twice because a couple of twelve-year olds in nineteen- and twenty-one-year-old bodies decided that the fraternity would get a bad reputation if he was in it. Who says that the Three Mile Island spill on Wednesday, March 28, was the stupidest thing that happened that week?

The Mixed Bag folder includes Tuesday, August 1, 1995, when he was on a retreat and someone had the nerve to tell him that he didn't have an intelligent looking face. People would only know he is intelligent by talking to him. Later at dinner, the retreat leader encouraged him by saying, "Anything is possible with you." If you read *Heal Your Memories, Change Your Life* you may recall the story on Saturday, August 25, 2012, when he and a lot of his family were at the beach. It was fun until his step grandson Trevor said, "Pop, your nose is bleeding." It had been a heck of a wave ride but it came with a price.

Frank Healy

If you have already read *Heal Your Memories, Change Your Life* you know that the man with all of these memories is me. If you haven't read my other book, you may have already guessed that this man is me. I was born with a Highly Superior Autobiographical Memory which means that I can remember every day of my life with near- perfect detail. While this is a gift when the days are good days, it can also be quite a burden when something bad happens. That is why I have dedicated my life to counseling and coaching work that helps people release their unhappy feelings from their memories and learn from their past. In *Heal Your Memories, Change Your Life* I provided many exercises to help the reader release the feelings they may be storing from negative memories. In this book, I'll give you the tools you need to learn from your memories so that you can turn them into positive experiences to draw from in your future.

Many of us who have Highly Superior Autobiographical Memory, including myself, have been on radio and talk shows. One of the mental gymnastics we are often asked to engage in is for someone else to name a date and then we go as far back into our memories as we can and describe what we were doing on that date, year by year. For example, here is my list of things for August 1, along with the folders they were in. Although I remember each year I have limited this list to significant events.

Monday, 1966, in the Fun to Remember folder, my family and I arrived in Sea Isle City, New Jersey, for vacation.

Tuesday, 1967, in the Mixed Bag folder, my family and I were on vacation again, but this year there were a lot of jellyfish in the water.

Friday, 1969, in the Fun to Remember folder, it was the final day of summer camp. We had a costume contest and I won the award for the silliest costume. I was wearing a devil costume with a clown mask.

The Ultimate Guide To Healing Your Past

Sunday, 1971, in the Fun to Remember folder, my dad and I took a nighttime walk on the beach in Sea Isle. It was foggy so it was the perfect setting for some deep discussion. That was usually how I bonded with my dad.

Thursday, 1974, in the Fun to Remember folder, it was a great day on the beach with some friends. One of the boys I met that day told me I was the best friend he ever had.

Friday, 1975, in the Mixed Bag folder, although it was a mixed experience, it was a very memorable day. We were leaving Sea Isle City after spending seven weeks there. We always started our vacation on the last day of school. It was sunny and the high temperature hit ninety-seven degrees. My mother and I traveled in one car while my father brought my brother and sister in his pickup truck. The radiator had a leak in it so we had to make frequent stops to refill the radiator with bottles of water that we had with us. In 1975, there were no cell phones so we couldn't call anyone for help – we had to keep driving. One of the stops we made to refill the radiator was in front of a junkyard where a man who had run for Congress and President was living in a tent. Being a fifteenyear-old kid with a thirst for adventure, I had hoped he would come out of his tent and we could meet him. That didn't happen, but we did make it home safely. It was a lifetime family memory and story to tell.

Monday, 1977, in the Fun to Remember folder, friends of the family were at our house visiting. I was a newly licensed driver and this was the first time I drove a group of kids somewhere. We went to the arcade and had a great time.

Wednesday, 1979, in the Pain in the Brain folder, I took my car to the garage for inspection and it failed. Months earlier, my friend had patched up some pipes but they were apparently illegal. It was expensive for the garage to replace the work my friend had done. Grrrr!

Frank Healy

Friday, 1980, in the Mixed Bag folder, people were being obnoxious at work. It was a stressful day at the office. That same night though, my mother noticed that I had lost some weight. I then began exercising more and lost sixty pounds over the next few months.

Saturday, 1981, in the Pain in the Brain folder, I remember working in a pharmacy that summer. The company car went dead in the parking lot of a high-rise condo complex. As if I wasn't feeling bad enough about the car, that day the pharmacist also said to me, "You are a lost cause."

Monday, 1988, in the Fun to Remember folder, I was starting a new job the next day. That evening I met my sister Jennifer at the local mall. We had dinner together and she helped me shop for clothes for the new job. I remember all the Oxford shirts I bought.

Tuesday, 1989, in the Fun to Remember folder, I was in graduate school for Counseling Psychology. In one of my classes, we watched a video of an obnoxious man in a counseling session. The class made jokes about it and we laughed quite a bit.

Wednesday, 1990, in the Pain in the Brain folder, unlike 1989, was the low point of my graduate school career. We had paired with other students and recorded videos of ourselves role playing in counseling sessions. On this day, my video was viewed and critiqued by my classmates. It is amazing how a group of kindhearted, save-the-world minded, and educated people can become the most rude and mean group of people when they critique their colleagues work. My first session on Wednesday, June 20, had gone well but for this one they came with their claws out and completely ripped it apart. I wasn't the only one to receive a bad critique, but it is never easy to hear bad remarks and criticism from classmates who you thought respected you.

Wednesday, 2001, in the Pain in the Brain folder, I was in the hospital with the worst case of summer pneumonia that the doctors had ever seen. **That evening I watched the six o'clock news on my little television over the bed. They reported that a twenty-seven-year-old football player on the Minnesota Vikings named Corey Stringer died of a respiratory disease early that morning. They showed a video of him working out at camp the previous day. Wow! I hope I get better. I was terrified that the same thing was going to happen to me.**

Monday, 2005, in the Fun to Remember folder, I was featured on the front page of the *Atlantic City Press* for my memory gift. The article was titled, "For Ocean City Man, Trip Down Memory Lane is a Marathon."

Tuesday, 2006, in the Mixed Bag folder, I was excited that my first blog was published on EZine Articles. My excitement was gone through once I tried to leave for work and my car wouldn't start.

Friday, 2014, in the Fun to Remember folder, my wife and I were sitting by the bay at my mother-in-law's house in Stone Harbor (rough life huh?). It was quiet at first, but then out of nowhere we heard one of the kids from the extended family, a sixteen-year-old girl who is as nice a young lady as you could ever meet, let out an ear deafening scream for her fourteenyear-old brother to keep his hands to himself.

There is one more folder I haven't told you about yet. I've named this folder Lessons from Memories. One of the ways I've found to cope with the bad feelings I experience from all of the bad memories I carry with me is to always identify at least one lesson I can learn from those experiences. This helps me to ensure that the same experience won't happen again if possible, or that if it does, it won't sting as badly. Lessons can be learned from good memories also to make them even better. Let me give you a few examples. First, we will look at the August 1 activities in the Pain in the Brain folder.

Frank Healy

In 1979, I learned from the failed car inspection to never let anyone but a Certified Licensed Mechanic work on my car. Some things really are best left to the professionals. Although I was angry at the time, I forgave my friend who wanted to play amateur mechanic. He is still a good friend and we both have many good memories together. This experience also taught me to take a more active approach to car maintenance, including changing the oil every five thousand miles as directed in the car manual.

In 1981, when the company car broke down in the condo parking lot, I learned that I do not have to blame myself for everything that goes wrong, especially with someone else's things. The car was theirs, not mine. It wasn't my fault.

In 1990, I learned that I should always come to class prepared. I had entered graduate school with the overly confident attitude that I already knew how to counsel since I had been doing it informally in the psychiatric hospital for two years. However, from this bloodbath experience, I also learned that not all people who counsel others had the title "Saint" in front of their name. Now that I'm out of school, I still make sure that I am prepared before I give a presentation at work or before book signings.

In 2001, I learned to be grateful for every day that I am still alive. After that hospitalization for pneumonia, I also learned to start taking better care of myself by getting more sleep, making healthier eating decisions, managing my stress, and other such things.

From these examples, you can see that there are some good and useful lessons to be learned from bad and unpleasant memories. Let's also see what we can learn from the memories in the Mixed Bag folder.

August 1, 1975, I learned from the experience of the radiator breaking to always be prepared for emergencies. Ironically, I also learned that when things go wrong it gives you a good story to tell for decades. When you think about it, which holidays, vacations, and times spent with friends and family are the most memorable? Chances are you will name the events where there were problems or when everything seemed to go wrong. At the time you probably thought, someday we will laugh about this. Those memories always seem to make the best stories. By the way, there is nothing wrong with laughing about it when it happens and not waiting for "someday."

Reflecting on the August 1, 1980, memory with the coworker that I had said was being obnoxious, I realized that I had been the one who started it. My coworker was only responding to what I had done and I really had no reason in this case to be upset with him.

Let's fast forward twenty-six years to another Mixed Bag memory on Tuesday, August 1, 2006. I had been considering a career in writing for many years. Then I heard about Ezine Articles. I wrote an article titled "My Extraordinary Memory Skills" and submitted it to Ezine. On July 31, they published my article and I learned that I could be a writer. This article then became the first chapter of a full book that I wrote called *Living With A Phenomenal Memory*.

In the old Peanuts comic strip, the main character, Charlie Brown, had a baseball team that always lost. After one game, the catcher named Schroeder told Charlie Brown that we learn more from losing than winning. Charlie retorted that he must be the smartest person in the world. But bad memories aren't the only memories that we can take lessons from. You can learn things from good memories, too, whether they are lessons that tell you what you should do the next time around, or just lessons that teach you more about who you are as a person and what you do or don't enjoy. Engaging in experiences such as these is called niche picking. A niche is something that you like and is a part of you.

Back in 1988 my parents moved to a new house. They had lived in a suburban, three-bedroom colonial since Friday, September 30,

Frank Healy

1966, when I was six years old, my brother Mark was four, and my sister Jennifer was still two months away from being born. Now my little sister was out of college and it was time for my dad to fulfill his dream of owning a farm.

For as long as I can remember, part of our dinner conversation consisted of my dad stating, "Let's get a farm," or, "When will we get the farm?" One night when my dad wasn't home, Wednesday, April 13, 1983, my sister, not wanting the routine to be lost in my dad's absence, said at the dinner table, "When I came home from the hospital after being born, my dad said, "When will we get the farm?" We all laughed.

Finally, in 1988 the stage was set and my dad bought his dream farm. One day my brother drove to see the area and the house where they had moved. When he was finished exploring the new territory, he said he had an incredible experience and decided he loves the country setting. That was his niche picking experience.

You may have had a niche picking experience the first time you went skiing or tried out for a part in a local show. Maybe it happened when you visited a new place and decided you would eventually move there. It can happen anywhere. The experience cannot be forced. It just happens naturally. You do not need to heal that memory just think of it as one in which you learned more about who you are.

The reverse is true, too. **I remember accounting class in high school. Perhaps surprisingly I found that class boring and devoid of any meaning. One would think that I would have liked it because the ledgers had numbers like the calendars. However, I discovered that it was not my field. I preferred subjects that required abstract thinking such as psychology, religion, and philosophy.**

Your niche picking or non-niche picking experiences should be based on how you feel. For example, I always enjoyed going to restaurants to eat but never liked working in restaurants. You might enjoy watching shows but maybe would never enjoy acting.

Another reason that it is important to choose your niches by how you feel is that too many people base their life decisions on what others tell them they should want or do. **Often if you ask a young adult what they want they look at you as if you were from Mars. Most young people have had their lives scripted for them and they have memories of being told what kind of career they should have, what kind of people they should be friends with, or what kind of person to marry, and they never reflect on what they actually want for themselves. You can use your memories of what you liked to avoid falling into this trap.**

Let's revisit the Fun to Remember folder and I'll show you examples of niche picking and how I learned from my good memories.

In 1966, after visiting Sea Isle City for vacation with my family, I learned that I love the shore. I eventually moved to the shore in 1997.

In 1967, I learned that I like swimming in the ocean so much that I don't even care if there are a ton of jellyfish around.

In 1971, I learned from the memory of bonding with my father that a dark and foggy beach is the perfect atmosphere for deep discussions.

In 1974, when I had a great day on the beach building a sandcastle with a group of kids, and there was a ten-year-old who told me I was his best friend, I learned that I am great with kids.

What did I learn from winning the costume contest as a devilish clown on August 1, 1969? Creativity with a unique angle wins the prize. This lesson has served me well in my writing career.

Frank Healy

How about when I thought I was such a big shot driving kids to an arcade on August 1, 1977? I use this memory to remind myself that even when I'm stuck in traffic, sometimes driving can be fun.

Clothing shopping with my sister on August 1, 1988, was good bonding. My siblings and I are still close, and it is fun when my lovely wife takes me shopping. It is not that I don't have a sense of fashion but it is always more fun to have company.

In the graduate class where we watched the obnoxious man in a counseling session and laughed as a group on August 1, 1989, I learned that having fun and being able to laugh with others is a necessity in life. In the field of counseling you have to be able to laugh. Laughing at life can be fun, too, and certainly helps to take the edge off of the heavier side of life.

On Friday, 2014, when I laughed at the young lady's outburst for her brother to keep his hands to himself, it was a reminder that even nice people need to let things out sometimes. The stereotype that nice people are not supposed to get angry is certainly unfair.

I have not always learned lessons from my memories immediately. For example, growing up I was always a quiet and shy kid. As I prepared to start my senior year in college in September, 1981, I thought about challenging the belief that I have to be quiet my whole life. I went through my marathon trip down memory lane. Was there ever a time in my life when I was fun and entertaining? I remembered on March 14 and 15, 1975, I played a comic relief character in our school play, *Get Witch Quick*. I was the gardener at a witch's college in Salem, Massachusetts, where the witch trials took place in the seventeenth century. Since my character did not know that the other students were witches, it made for some hysterical lines. My part in that play popped up six-and-a-half years later and I drew from that experience to now become the one who catches

people off guard and says something funny with dry humor rather than being the quiet one all the time.

You too can learn from your old memories. That is exactly what this book is about – taking the past, no matter how long ago, and learning how to do better in life now. As you discover things about yourself you may regret that you did not learn the lesson years ago, but don't worry about it – it's never too late. From a spiritual perspective, many believe that our time on earth is meant for us to learn lessons. If we do not learn the lesson the first time, we will have harsher experiences until we do learn. **For example, if we keep entering into abusive relationships, we will continue to develop more abusive relationships until we work on our self-esteem and learn to set limits on abusive people.**

Perhaps the logo of this book could be, "It's never too late to learn from a memory."

Exercise 1 – Let's Learn From Some Memories

You will need a pen or pencil and a notebook, or a blank Word document on your computer.

1. Pick a memory that was not very pleasant. It does not have to be the worst thing that ever happened to you, but it should be something that made you sad or uncomfortable.

2. List anything that you may have already learned from that memory.

3. Now list some things you could learn now. Even if it is just one thing, it is still worth the exercise.

4. Now pick a happy memory. It could be a good time with friends or family, or an activity that you excelled at.

5. List something you learned from the good memory. It could be that you learned you like going to a certain place, that you enjoy

certain types of people, that you are good at something, or anything of your choosing.

6. List the additional things you could learn.

Congratulations! You have now completed the first exercise. You've learned something new about yourself and now you are better prepared for your future!

It probably did not take you long to do this exercise, but for some people, I know that a few minutes can seem like too much to spare for things that aren't in your daily routine. The next chapter will help guide you through what you can do if you feel that you just don't have the time to reflect on your experiences in life.

Chapter 2

What About CEO'S and Soccer Moms? We Don't Have The Time To Look Back And Learn From Our Memories

Recently, a lady who I went to school with sent me a Facebook message. She said that she has been receiving my newsletters and would like to do the exercises and activities that I provide in them so that she can be healed from her past memories, but she doesn't seem to have the time. She explained that she has been in and out of the hospital for surgeries related to cancer. She also explained that there are some other stressors in her life and that with everything going on, she just can't get the exercises done.

When I used to teach General Psychology and College Skills, I always had the students go through a time management exercise. The students were required to make logs of how they spent their time each day. They would list their activities and how long each would take and then we would review them as a class to discuss ways that we could improve their time management skills. In one of these classes, there was a young man who shared that masturbation was one of the activities that he blocked time for in his day. Without flinching I said, "We all have our priorities."

What I learned from that Tuesday, October 26, 2004, memory was that I can handle obnoxiousness without flinching. There was an evaluator in the class that day as well who commented on my evaluation form that I handled the situation well. What *you* can learn from this is that you can make the exercises in this book a priority worth working into your schedule. If you want to learn and grow you will make the time. If you read my free report entitled, "5 Exercises You Can Do Today To Heal The Past," then you know that the exercises do not take long to do – twenty to thirty minutes each at the most.

Often I hear my clients say that they are too busy to go out to dinner, or to the casinos, or to the movies, or to talk to their kids. I usually tell them, "Wow, if you are that busy, you must be a master of scheduling. Schedule your leisure time into your schedule and it will be just as much fun." In this case, I would add that you should schedule some time also to make these exercises a priority.

Exercise 2 – You Have The Time

You will need a pen and paper, or an Excel Spreadsheet.

1.   Across the top of a clean piece of paper or a new Excel spreadsheet, write the days of the week. Down the left side of the paper or spreadsheet, write the times of the day in one hour increments (6AM, 7AM, 8AM, and so on).

2.   Beginning the next morning and continuing for the next week until the chart you created is full, write down how you spent your time in the appropriate blocks of the chart. For example, if you went shopping on Friday at three in the afternoon, then write shopping in the 3PM block for Friday. If you are filling the chart in after the day is over and you can't quite remember specific times, a best estimate is fine.

3.   At the end of the week, make some time to reflect on the information in your chart. Are there any activities that you didn't

realize you were spending so much time doing? Are there any activities that you might be able to eliminate or spend less time on? Is there anything you wanted to do but didn't get done, like the exercises in this book? Is there anything you did on a certain day or at a certain time that might have taken less time if you did it on another day or at a different time? Shopping at three in the afternoon on a Friday when there are a ton of people in the grocery store for example can take longer than shopping on a Tuesday night at seven or eight when there aren't as many people there. Was there something that you could have skipped doing so that you would have had time to do some of the exercises in this book?

4.   After you've had some time to reflect on your chart, prioritize some time to continue reading this book and to do the exercises. Healing the hurt from your memories and learning from them is worth the time now to create a brighter future for yourself.

Now you know how to make the time, but maybe you are thinking, what's the point of learning from events that happened long ago? If I did not learn the lesson then, why would I learn it now?

In the last chapter I gave an example of how I took a memory and learned from it six years later. Recall my role in the school play March 14 and 15, 1975. Then in 1981, I decided to use that offbeat, dry-humored role as a social role in my everyday life.

Your brain is always trying to help you think and to solve problems. When a memory pops into your head, there is a reason that particular memory surfaced rather than another. Sometimes it could be a good memory. For example, on Tuesday, July 16, 1974, when I was fourteen, I rode my bike past a cobblestone parking lot. I had a déjà vu experience as I recalled being in that parking lot as a small child. This was before my ability to recall dates for every day, but I do remember sitting on the hatchback of a car with my parents changing my clothes after a fun day at the beach.

Your brain gives you good memories and feelings when you are in a situation similar to something that happened in your past. Your brain will do the same for bad memories and feelings. Any time you feel anxious, sad, or just that vague feeling that something is not right, there is a high chance that your brain will recall a memory from your past that left you upset in some way. This is the brain just doing its job – trying to solve problems.

Imagine that at a previous job, your boss called you in the office and told you that you were fired. Now its years later and the boss at your current job approaches you with an angry or concerned look on their face and says that he or she wants to speak with you. Immediately you get tense and have a flashback of that other time when you were fired.

Sometimes the association of one memory to another might not be so obvious. Maybe when your parents argued they followed up over the next couple of days with the silent treatment and it always felt tense in the house. As a child you may have blamed yourself for their silence. Children have a tendency to exaggerate their impact on their world. Now as an adult you get very uncomfortable with silence when you are with your friends or significant other and you can't help but think that you did something wrong.

The brain tries to solve current problems by reminding you of similar scenarios in the past. The specific memories that the brain recalls in these situations are the ones you need to heal and learn from. If you didn't learn something at the time the memory actually happened, perhaps it just wasn't the right time to do so, or perhaps you were too young to really think about the event in a logical way. You don't need to be concerned if the right memory surfaces, nor if you need to heal every one. The right memories will surface at the right times.

Now that you know how to find the time to heal your bad memories and learn lessons from them, the next chapter will show you how to turn those bad experiences into good experiences in the future.

Chapter 3

Take Your Learnings Light Years Further

How would you like to beam proudly as you hold your college degree in your hand? Now you can have the job of your dreams and conquer the world. You can get any job that the world has to offer. But maybe you don't want any job in the world. Maybe what you want is a boss who is a passiveaggressive control freak. This boss of your dreams must immediately shoot down any ideas you have about new projects or process improvements. As a matter of fact, hopefully they will shoot you down before you can even finish your sentences. They must also be willing to attack you at all staff meetings in front of all of your coworkers.

Or maybe your dream job is an administrative position in an office filled with twelve-year olds in twentysomething bodies. Preferably the rest of the staff will have a tendency to make up stories and backstab. If you dare correct them they have a right to twist everything around and say it is your fault. They must have cliques and talk about going out on Friday nights in front of you after they didn't invite you. You can be friends with some of the staff but only ones who never hesitate to tell you everything that people are gossiping about, especially if that gossip contains bits and pieces of how incompetent and stupid you are. After all, these people are your friends.

Perhaps you know you want to work in a building that looks like it has been condemned for at least twenty years. Location, location,

location! There must be regular shootouts in the neighborhood, litter all over the sidewalks, and graffiti on the trash cans. There must be an annual evaluation where your boss makes sure that you know you are lucky to still have your job.

Now that you have some ideas for your career, let's get the wonderful world of dating straight. First dates must be in restaurants where you arrive early and make all the tedious arrangements. Then when your date walks in, he or she must scream, "Well don't just stand there, get to the table!" It will help in the future for this person to always say you never do anything for them after the two of you just came back from a relaxing and beautiful weekend at the shore that you planned and paid for. If it just so happens that this person has to go to the hospital for a night or two and you read to them to help pass some of the time, he or she must tell you that their roommate's visitor could not wait for you to shut up. **This person must have no investment in life. They must yell at you if you dare suggest that they do more with their life or get a job rather than being an entitled-to-be-retired person at twenty-something years old. After all, this person had a rough week in college once and that just wasn't the path for them. The best memory will be when you paid for dinner on your own birthday.** Also, given all the different conversational styles out there, perhaps your absolute favorite is when you are constantly interrupted and the other person changes topics midstream. Oh to have a partner like that!

These examples are hypothetical. If you can relate to any of these scenarios or have been in any of these situations then you know that they are absolutely not what you want in life. Hopefully you had fun and got a laugh out of it.

In the examples above, there were many things that no one would ever want to happen. Unfortunately, maybe you have had one of these experiences or you can remember another bad event that did happen but you wish you could erase. One of the best ways to learn from a memory that you do not like is to see it as a live demonstration of what you don't want. In many ways, life shows us what we do and don't want and you can turn any memory into a lesson of do this or don't do that.

So now you know that you don't want a job where you are always the scapegoat for an arrogant and inconsiderate boss, and you also know that you don't want an abusive partner who doesn't appreciate a thing in their life. Intellectually, you know that these would be bad situations, but how do you turn that knowledge into motivation for going after what you *do* want?

Some experts say that all motivation comes from moving away from pain and moving towards pleasure. If you read *Heal Your Memories, Change Your Life*, you know that I am not a fan of pain. It is much better to heal emotional pain than to live with it. In my expertise, I will instead say to you: rah rah rah! Feel the pain of your memories, heal them, learn from them, and you will move towards a more fulfilling life.

Here is where you might run into some trouble though. Our brains are completely obedient to what we put in them. In the 90s, there was an expression about computers, "Garbage in, garbage out." In other words, if you put bad programming or commands into a computer, you will get a useless output. Perhaps not surprisingly our brains work the same way. If we think negative thoughts or dwell on negative experiences, we are more likely to produce more unhappy experiences.

The classic example of this is the person who goes from one abusive relationship or marriage to another. When they first meet someone, their wishful thinking or blind love tells them that this one is different. However, as the months go by they ignore the telltale signs that this one will be the same and soon they are being abused again. The problem was that all they could think about was how they didn't want to be abused and they didn't think at all about what it was that they do want from a relationship.

Minor tragedies happen every day. A student decides that they are not going to fail another test but they keep failing. An athlete thinks that if they dwell on their mistakes they will know what to do next time so that they don't make the same mistakes again but at the next game, they make the same mistake. When you dwell of what you don't want, you actually wind up manifesting it because you are feeding garbage into your brain.

How does this relate to healing your memories, or learning from them? You can take a memory of something that you didn't like or something that you definitely don't want to happen again and focus on the opposite so that you aren't putting more garbage into your brain and consequently your life. Healing from your memories and learning from them helps you to bring about the things in your life that you want to happen and enjoy.

Example 1- Find The Opposite

• After being on a date with someone totally obnoxious, you've thought about the situation and have learned that you know you want to date someone who has manners and treats you with respect.

• After going bowling with some friends every Friday for the past two months and getting the lowest score out of everyone each time, you now know you need to find another hobby, unless you are a good sport and like bowling anyway.

• After being told by your parents that if you don't get into medical school you will have to pay back the tuition they paid for your undergraduate degree, you decide that you really want to be a doctor and will work as hard as you can to make sure you get into medical school.

• After working many summers with your dad on construction sites with people yelling and cursing at you for everything you do, you learn that this is not the life for you and that you will be going to college next semester.

Please note that some of these examples can go both ways. I have a friend whose parents pressured him to go to college but he was always a better craftsman than a student. He went to college for one semester without ever purchasing a textbook. Finally his guidance counselor told him to stop wasting his time and money and just drop out. He took their advice and he has been a successful electrician and house builder ever since. Then there are some people who live at the shore where I do and never go to the beach. A friend of ours tells people like that to move to Nebraska. It's all about what you want.

There is a big difference between knowing what you want and don't want intellectually and really feeling it. Emotions are what drive people to live their best life, so you need to not only learn from your memories by thought but feel the feelings from the experiences also. The next exercise will show you how to do this.

Exercise 3 – Feel The Difference

You will need some quiet and undisturbed time, a comfortable place to sit or lie down, and your pen and notepad, or Word document.

1.   Pick a memory where you did not like what was happening. This memory should be a situation that you were in for at least a few months. It could be a job you did not like, a class that you did not enjoy, a bad relationship, or a place you lived that you did not like. Pick any memory in which you weren't happy.

2.   Write down all of the aspects of the memory that you did not like. It could be the work you did, the people you were with, the way you were treated, the lack of pleasurable surroundings. For example, maybe you are artistic and you once had a job in a basement that was dimly lit and poorly decorated.

3.   Write the opposite of the situation. Use Example 1 for the general idea.

4.   Now you will use your imagination. Get into a relaxing position. It could be lying down or sitting comfortably in a chair.

5.   Take a couple of deep breaths. Remind yourself that this is your time to introduce yourself to what you want. Imagine relaxing deeper and deeper into the chair or whatever you are laying on.

6.   Imagine yourself experiencing all of the things that you put on your list in Step 3. This could include being in your ideal relationship, having an art gallery, or playing music instead of participating in sports. This is for you to imagine and feel what you want.

7.   Take as much time as you want to stay in your world where everything is exactly how you want it to be.

8.   When you are ready, open your eyes and come back into the room.

Congratulations! You have now completed another exercise. Learning from your memories can now seem more real and meaningful to you than it would if you just intellectually grasped the concepts. You now have an idea of how you can use your memories and learn from them to create the life you want.

What if you know you've had the life you wanted in the past but now the fun and joy are gone? How can you learn from those memories? Keep reading.

Chapter 4

If Those Were The Days,
What Is Good About Today?

Many of my clients suffer from depression. While depression can have a physical side to it such as imbalanced neurotransmitters or vitamin deficiencies that may require medication, often it is caused by the perception that life is not as good as it used to be or as good as it should be. Here are two examples of how these perceptions can happen.

Example 2 - Major Ways Your Life May Not Seem Worthwhile Anymore

•   I used to be active in my local bar's baseball and football teams, but now I'm unable to keep my balance and can't walk without the assistance of a walker.

•   I used to be a real tiger in the business world. Now I am retired and Bingo and Gin Rummy just don't fulfill my ambitious and competitive nature.

•   My spouse and I used to have intellectual discussions that would last for hours. Now my spouse is living with a diagnosis of dementia.

•   I had a few good friends growing up, but they all went out of state for college. Talking to them on Facebook is not the same as spending real time with them.

- We devoted our lives to the kids. Now we have an empty nest.

- My spouse died and even though we were married for twenty years, their family does not include me in anything.

- When I was in my twenties, I knew where every bar was within fifty miles. Now I know where every funeral home is in the same radius.

Example 3 – Minor Ways Life Might Seem Not As Good

- I used to go to all these parties but now the friend who invited me moved away.

- I used to be popular in school and was invited to all the parties. Now my coworkers ignore me and I don't get invited out after work.

- We can't go on a vacation this year because my wife is sick, or we can't afford it.

- We can't spend the summer at the shore anymore because we rent out our shore house to pay for college tuition.

Whether or not you think that your memories of better times will ever repeat themselves, you can still learn from them. Whenever you feel sad or depressed because you've lost something, thinking about what need or want was met in the better time that is not being met now can help you to identify what you need to do to restore the fun in your life.

Let's look at the previous examples and think of which needs were met. Then we will think of how the person can meet their needs now in a different way.

Example 4 – Identify Needs And How To Meet Them

1. The person who used to be athletic but now needs the help of a walker to get around has needs for physical activity, involvement with others, and the joys of competing.

Coaching a local sports team can fulfill two of these needs – the need for involvement and the joys of competition. The person's doctor or physical therapist could prescribe an exercise program within their physical abilities in order to satisfy their need for physical activity.

2.   I used to be a tiger in the business world. Now my excitement is going to the mall or playing Bingo and Gin Rummy. (I have nothing against Gin Rummy and I do not want any card players associations coming after me to ban the sale of this book. Really card games are okay if that is what you are into.)

This person has a strong need for achievement. They could join the local Chamber of Commerce or run for local office. Maybe they could become an advisor to Future Business Leaders. I have just one word of warning: if they were to choose the government option, government officials play lots of cards.

3.   My spouse and I used to have intellectual discussions that would last for hours. Now my spouse is living with a diagnosis of dementia.

If this describes you, you have a strong need for intellectual stimulation and connection to others. Join a book club or some other organization where you can have these needs met while someone stays with your spouse. Meanwhile, your spouse may feel the same way. They know something is wrong and feel confused and frustrated about it. Have intellectual discussions with them anyway and do not correct them if they make an erroneous statement. Let them feel that they are still intelligent.

4.   You devoted all of your time to your children. Now you have an empty nest and feel that nobody needs you anymore.

The person in this example has the need for a purpose in their life. When your whole purpose in life is to take care of others it is called codependency. People who have codependency have no sense of who they are, what they like, or what they are good at. For example, the codependent person would not define themselves as smart, attractive, Christian, a nurse, or a computer operator. Outside of their kids, this person has no identity. If this describes you it may be helpful to look back at your memories before marriage and children. What did you excel in? What did you enjoy doing? Consider volunteering or going to school for a helping profession. My recommendation is that you exercise both of these options. You need to discover who you are but continue to take care of others. This would be an excellent time to start niche picking as described in the first chapter.

5.   I had a few good friends growing up, but they all went out of state for college. Talking to them on Facebook is not the same as spending real time with them.

This person has a need to be with people and to spend meaningful time with others. It can be hard to make new friends, but someone in this situation could recall how they met their old friends and put forth the same effort with new people.

I realize that meeting new people is scary for many. People tend to forget things they have done successfully in the past if they haven't done it in a long time. Remember that you have made new friends in the past – you can do it again!

6.   My spouse died and now their family does not invite me to events. I guess they never liked me to begin with.

This person feels hurt because their needs for love and acceptance are no longer met. People experience hurt when someone else does not meet their need for love and acceptance that they thought they would.

28

When people lose someone, especially a loved one, they can become temporarily neurotic. They may have bizarre reasons for why they might stop doing something. For example, your spouse's family might not want to see you because seeing you reminds them of the fact that their loved one died. I know that does not help the hurt, but please take comfort in knowing that in this instance, they are not excluding you because they don't like you.

The first thing you could do is to find out why they don't include you. Of course this is scary because you risk being told that they don't want you around, but if you have other supportive people in your life draw on them as an emotional buffer. If you don't have family or support, you can join a church or rekindle old friendships.

7.   When I was in my twenties I knew where every bar was within fifty miles. Now I am in my seventies and I know where every funeral home is in the area.

Everyone wants to live and enjoy life. So be glad you are still alive and give yourself a good laugh.

Now here are the situations that are more disappointments than devastations.

8.   I used to go to parties all the time. Now the friend who invited me moved away.

These days you can friend the friend on Facebook and find the other partiers through their friends. Don't say that you are not good at that stuff. It is not hard to do. People in general need to connect and they have the same want and need you do for connection and fun.

9.   I used to be popular in school. Now my coworkers don't bother with me and I don't even get invited out.

Your need to feel important, accepted, and connected was met well while you were in school but not now that you are in the working world. You could look at your school memories to figure out what made you popular. Remember though that the qualities that make a person popular in school do not always work in the adult world. It may behoove you to observe adults who are well liked and see how they charm others.

One theory of popularity suggests that the kids who observe what works in others and what does not work is the key. Then they adapt the behaviors that work. It is not necessarily the athletic boy or the pretty girl. If you were popular you must know what works for kids and teenagers. Use your observation skills and apply them to coworkers and other adults.

10.   We can't go on vacation this year because my spouse is sick, or we don't have the money this year.

This is a good situation to apply the Richard London theory that you'll read about in a later chapter of "All problems are temporary." It could be a time of selfexploration. How can we have fun closer to home? Maybe if you can't go to Europe this year you can go to your local beach, go on some day trips, or join your local swim club.

11.   We can't spend summer at the shore now because we are renting our house to tenants to pay for my sibling's college.

This is an experience I had. During my high school years, in the summers of 1974 through 1978, my family spent the summers in our house in Sea Isle City, New Jersey. After 1978, we stopped going because we had to rent out the house to raise tuition money for college. The shore had always been my release from the pressures of school and social life. Not going was traumatic but I discovered other things I liked doing, such as ball games, museums in the city, and swimming in pools. Eventually I moved to the shore anyway.

These examples illustrate that when something ends in your life it helps to always think about what needs were met and how you can meet them now in a different way. There is the old adage, "When one door closes another one opens." You can actively make the right door open by reflecting on your experiences and learning what your needs and wants are. **Exercise 4 – How Are Your Wants And Needs Being Met** You will need pen and paper, or your Word document.

1.   Think of a time in your life when you felt very happy. Pick a specific situation, preferably one that occurred frequently.

2.   Write down the scenario in detail. How old were you? Where was it? Who were you with? How did you feel?

3.   Write what needs you felt were met then. Did you feel important and respected? Did you feel that you had something to strive for or to care about? Did you feel connected to others? Were you having fun?

4.   Now write how those needs are being met in the present. You may need to think about all corners of your life. For example, work may fulfill your need for accomplishment but your friends would fulfill your need for connection.

5.   Write any needs that you feel are no longer being met but were met in that special time. Maybe work does not fulfill your need for purpose and accomplishment the way it used to. Maybe your social life is not as good as it was.

6.   Now brainstorm some ideas of how you can meet these needs now.

Hopefully as you read this chapter and did the exercise you were able to learn what some of your own needs and wants are.

Although everyone will have different wants and needs, there are some basic ones that everyone seems to have. People have a need for acceptance, a need for achievement, a need for significance, a need for connectedness, a need for life balance, and a need for stimulation. Sometimes you have a need to be alone and other times a need to connect with others.

Ironically, these needs seem to contradict each other. The need for privacy contradicts the need to connect with others. The need for outstanding achievement contradicts the need to blend in. There are many examples of contradicting needs. Sometimes we need to accept the fact that we humans are complex creatures. The more complex we are the more we seem contradictory.

Some people have less of one need and more of another. For example, research scientists or computer geeks (all of the computer geeks I know are okay with being called computer geeks) have a stronger need for intellectual achievement than for connection with others. They often feel more comfortable and more in control of a keyboard and a software program than they do a social situation. Their need for connection is often satisfied by their families and a couple of close friends.

Someone else might have a stronger need for connection and social stimulation but their achievement need is satisfied by organizing and throwing a successful party. We are all different in our needs and satisfactions. It is important for your happiness to look at your memories and learn from them what your specific needs are.

If you are having trouble thinking of things that you could learn from your memories, the next few chapters will show you how a few people overcame incredible obstacles and improved the quality of their lives from the lessons they learned from their experiences. Some of these amazing people even found their life purpose through their trauma. If it were not for their bad memories, they would not have become the people they are today.

Chapter 5

Therapy Always Includes A Personal Touch, Even With Animals

Kelly Meister-Yetter had anxiety and trouble trusting people. Her childhood memories included ongoing sexual abuse from her father from age two through twelve. She was a very shy child who lacked self-confidence and the ability to trust people. After all, if you can't trust your parents, who can you trust?

By early adulthood Kelly realized that her anxiety and lack of assertiveness were going to cause problems for her if she did not get help. **She started therapy and tried several therapists until she found one that helped her. She was glad that she kept trying as talk therapy helped tremendously. She also tried anti-psychotic and antiseizure medications until she found the ones that helped her.**

Additionally, Kelly tried some unconventional therapies. EMDR is a therapy that was created in the late 80s. The acronym means Eye Movement Desensitization and
Reprogramming. Typically how it works is the therapist asks the client to recall a traumatic memory which the client has strong feelings about. The therapist instructs the client to follow their finger

movement. The finger moves like a windshield wiper on a car and the client's eyes go back and forth while they recall the memory and re-experience the feelings.

How can moving a finger back and forth while someone feels anxious, sad, or angry help them? Moving the eyes realigns the nervous system so the client will no longer feel the painful feeling. Therefore, they lose the ability to feel the memory even if they can't lose the memory itself.

Kelly received EMDR therapy but it did not help her. **It is common for someone seeking therapy to try several ones. Some help, others don't.**

At this time, Kelly became interested in animals. She had always liked horses and tried a unique kind of self-help therapy called Equine Assisted Therapy. Her goal in this therapy was to improve her communication skills and she benefitted.

Kelly was an animal lover. She joined an animal rescue squad and discovered that she loved helping animals. It took the focus off of her issues and brought her tremendous satisfaction.

Few of us can completely take the focus off ourselves even when we help others. Most of us desire appreciation and reciprocated love when we give. It is just human nature. For Kelly, part of her love of animals is that they gave back unconditionally. If you have ever heard someone say that they like dogs better than people, you understand. You go outside for a minute to get something out of the car and your dog jumps on you with the same enthusiasm as if you had been gone for a week.

When I talked to Kelly, I told her a true story of my family. My parents had a Standard Schnauzer, Sammy, who liked five people in the world, us, tolerated a few more, and barked at every other living thing. The day before she was put to sleep we showered her with attention and had a dinner in her honor. For the next week we took turns offering therapy to each other.

Kelly shared that she remembers that when favorite pets died, she became sadder than when some relatives died. She laughed as she said this.

I am not implying here that people are bad. I have spent my career helping them and caring about them. The implication is that animals give you unconditional love. If you can find a fellow homo sapien who does likewise, you are truly blessed.

As the title of this chapter suggests, sometimes therapy works better when you add self-discovery and find something that brings you joy unique to your personality. Kelly found a way of life that served her. Someone else might prefer sports, cycling, plants, reading, designing video games, visiting historical sites or volunteering in one. The list is endless. **The point is that memory healing works better when you discover who you are, and simply do what you love.**

Kelly has published some books, *Crazy Critter Lady* and *No Better Medicine*, and she has a website at www.crazycritterlady.com.

While Kelly found a lifestyle that served her, sometimes when you are young you think you have already found your niche but then something happens that causes you to have to rethink your priorities. If you read *Heal Your Memories, Change Your Life*, you recall two people who were confidently moving on with their lives but then had to change their priorities. They were Kit the juggler and Nancy the student. The next chapter shares a story of a man who also had to reorganize his life after a tragic accident.

Chapter 6

All Problems Are Temporary

Richard London was a confident young man in college. He was a handsome ambitious nineteen-year-old man who was studying for a career in law enforcement so he could become a police officer and eventually work for the FBI. Life was good and if there were any problems, Richard considered them temporary.

On Monday, November 10, 1975, gale force winds struck the Great Lakes. The SS Edmund Fitzgerald sank and twentynine crewmen were killed.

Three nights later, Thursday, November 13, Rich rode his motorcycle to his girlfriend's house. Although there were no gale force winds that night, there was a bad driver on the road who hit Rich's motorcycle. His leg was damaged so badly that it required multiple operations and plenty of hospital time over the next few months. His career in law enforcement went down with the ship.

Although he was disappointed that he could not be a police officer, Rich continued in college and decided to change his major to computers. He graduated and founded three computer companies. The years went by. **In 2002 at forty-six years old, Richard took a class in Kenpo, a Japanese martial art that combines Karate, Judo, and other martial arts. His leg began to bother him as an after effect of the motorcycle injury. Then the following year, he was diagnosed with prostate cancer. Rich did everything he** needed to heal. He ate right, took the medicine he was prescribed, and maintained his positive attitude. Seeing all problems as temporary was useful to him during this trying time. Rich has now been a cancer survivor for almost twelve years.

Sometimes things seem to happen one after the other. In 2005, Rich developed Parkinson's Disease. Since Parkinson's is considered incurable, looking at this problem as temporary contradicted all of the evidence. Rich again did everything he could to get well. In the midst of taking care of himself, he also decided to help other people with Parkinson's by starting a nonprofit organization. Helping people was his way of making it temporary.

Sometimes serendipitous things happen when a memory seems bad. Rich did not stay with the girlfriend he had in college but met another lady years later. He is happily married to a woman who would not have married him if he worked in law enforcement. She did not want to spend her life worrying if her husband would be killed on the job.

Rich has now expanded his role in helping people. He has published three books, including *A Handbook For Life* and *A Handbook For Happiness*. He has a DVD and three self-help audio CDs. You can order all of these products on www.AHandbookForLife.com. He uses his memories of injury and illness to help everyone see that a problem can be temporary.

Example 5 –What Kinds Of Problems Are Temporary?

• An illness where you miss work and have to stop your life for a few days. **Don't worry, you will catch up.**
• A bad date, even if it seems like the night will never be over. **Check for more compatible matches online or talk to your friends about who they know.**

•   Being blackballed from a Greek organization. **Try again or find other friends, and forget what any of the ones who blackballed you said about you. They are the victim, not you.**

•   Financial difficulties that force you to cancel your upcoming vacation and also make your kid pay for their own college tuition. **You will go on vacation again eventually, and your kid will learn self-reliance.**

•   The sports team you play for makes it to the championship game but then lost. **It was still fun to play.** ☐ You are stuck at a job you dislike. **You can look for a new job, do what you can to change the job you are in, or you can change your attitude about it.**

If you have been through any of these situations, you know that you survived and coped. I often tell my clients in crisis to look back and remember if they ever had a similar situation. How did they cope with it before? For example, they may have had a fight with their spouse or another family member, they may have had an episode of depression, or they may have had a previous job loss. When they recall how they survived something similar, they feel better and are more confident that they can survive their current crisis. Additionally I help them recall how they coped with the situation and then discuss how they can use the same skills now.

Some of the clients who I coach or counsel are in therapy for a short time because they just need to cope with a specific situation, a temporary problem, such as their children's bad behavior or an unsupportive spouse. Often they are helped by learning different behaviors. Sometimes if they have memories of when things worked better they just need to recall them and return to the behaviors and attitudes that helped them before. Conversely, if they have never coped well before they need to learn new skills, such as learning to view the issue from a temporary perspective like Rich.

Most of us were raised with the idea that the key to accomplishing what you want is to work hard. Even then you still risk that your efforts will be a waste, but you will increase your chances if you work hard and take the right actions. Our next story is about a woman who overcame a debilitating physical illness using visualizations and the right actions.

You can access Richard's website www.AHandbookForLife.com and get his eBooks and free newsletter.

Chapter 7

Visualizing Your Way to Good Health

Amy was four years into her marriage and pregnant with her first child in 1978. She and her husband had many friends. They had a beautiful home and it seemed that it was a healthy pregnancy. They excitedly planned a natural birth.

The first trimester blended into the second. However, Amy noticed that her morning sickness had not stopped and it was still lasting all day. Morning sickness is called morning sickness because the pregnant mother feels sick and nauseous in the morning. It happens because the body rids itself of teratogens, which are agents that could harm the growing fetus.

Hoping for a quick cure, Amy talked to her gynecologist about the sickness. Instead of reassuring her that things were okay, the doctor sent her to her gastroenterologist. This doctor told her it was inflammation of the intestines or Crohn's disease, and it was incurable.

Amy cried for three days. Then for the next month or two she sat around with her gloomy thoughts and felt depressed and scared with her baby growing inside of her. Would the baby be okay? Will I be able to take care of it? Am I going to be in pain for the rest of my life? On and on the same thoughts sent her further into a spiral of anxiety, self-doubt, pity, and depression.

In recent years there has been a lot of emphasis on visualizing and picturing yourself as already having the results you want. In 2006, the movie *The Secret* came out. In case you haven't seen the movie, here is the gist of it. It reveals a secret idea that government officials, rulers, church leaders and other elite people kept from the masses for centuries. The idea they didn't want anyone to know is that everything we have in our life we attracted to ourselves by our thoughts and feelings. It is called the Law of Attraction. Since the release of this movie, the Law of Attraction has been a big factor in the self-help movement.

Amy's sister gave her a book titled *Three Magic Words* by U.S. Anderson. It explained the now well known Law of Attraction. Amy took it to heart and began meditating daily. As she meditated she visualized total health. She believed so strongly in the potential of this approach that she pleaded with her brother-in-law who also had Crohn's disease to change his diet and his priorities. He chose instead to continue following the route of traditional medicine, but this didn't discourage Amy and she continued with the alternative therapy.

Believing she could now recover, she talked to her doctor about eating right. She began eating all the right foods. Her baby was born healthy and later she had another one.
Soon she had no more signs of Crohn's but she continued to eat healthy, meditate, and visualize.

Years earlier, the writer Norman Cousins was diagnosed with a rare disease called Ankylosing Spondylitis. He was told he only had a few months to live. In those days there was no Redbox for movie rentals and no way to download movies from the internet. However, Norman decided to take control of his recovery. He checked out of the hospital against medical advice and went to a hotel room where he watched comedy shows, The Marx Brothers movies, read comic books, and wrote his own jokes. He laughed all day. The old expression, "Laughter is the best medicine," applied here. However, Norman told reporters that it was taking control of his recovery that helped him the most.

After a month in the hotel room Norman returned to the hospital for a checkup. The doctors found no sign of the illness. Norman lived for many more years.

Amy's story is no less miraculous. Visualizing, eating right, and taking control of her healing all helped her recover. Taking control stopped her from feeling like a victim.

Now, decades later she is healthy, has a son and a daughter who are healthy young adults, and she shows no traces of Crohn's Disease. This is very good for someone who once had an allegedly incurable disease.

From this traumatic memory Amy learned that:

- **Setbacks do not mean failure.**
- **Perseverance gets you there.**
- **Stay positive and focus only on the end result with determination and conviction.**
- **The difference between try and triumph is a little umph.**
- **This was the best thing that happened to her because it opened a whole new path for her.**

Today Amy is a therapist. She became interested in therapy when she went to seminars that all expressed the "I can" attitude. She teaches that anything is possible. Amy still meditates. She laughed when I asked her if she is still as careful about her healthy eating. She replied, "Most of the time."

Amy Sherman, MA, has a master's degree in Counseling Psychology. She is the founder of the Baby Boomers' Network

Frank Healy

(www.yourbabyboomersnetwork.com) and the author of *99 Things Women Wish They Knew Before Dating After 40, 50 and Yes, 60!* She can be reached at amybethsherman@gmail.com.

As Amy, Richard, and Kelly overcame challenges of a specific nature, sometimes you will have different memories to learn from at specific times in your life. Our next story is of a remarkable lady who overcame childhood trauma, physical illness, and a bad marriage and is now living an incredible life.

Chapter 8

You Hold The Keys To Your Journey, No Matter Where You Were Before

Angi grew up during the 1970s in a home that regularly involved episodes of rage by her father. An alcoholic, her birth father was physically and emotionally abusive to her and her mother. In the 1970s, it was not taboo to hit or whip your children. Her mother was a narcissist. She worked nights at the local hospital and slept all day. A regular routine involved eating take out for dinner only. Angi never recalled her mother cooking a meal and the kitchen was barren of food, resulting in scavenging or routinely relying on neighbors or schoolmates for meals.

Angi vividly recalls that it was around the time when she was in fifth grade that she realized her household was abnormal and that other families did not exhibit alcoholism, rage, and physical or mental abuse. Her father moved to Indiana immediately following high school graduation. Her paternal grandparents never exhibited any signs of physical abuse or dysfunctional behaviors. Unfortunately, the fact that they lived out of state only allowed her to stay with them during the summer months. The normalcy during these summer visits greatly impacted her views of love and the

44

importance of stopping this cycle of abuse from continuing in her adult life.

At the age of ten, her baby sister was born. Angi recalls her father bringing her to the hospital to see her mother and new sister, but not before stopping by the local liquor store. Her father drank a large amount of alcohol and showed up at the hospital in a drunken stupor.

Then, when Angi was fourteen her parents divorced. Her father immediately remarried a woman he had previously dated during a trial separation when Angi was three years old.

At the age of fourteen, despite Angi's abusive childhood, nothing could have prepared her for the abuse and manipulation she underwent from her stepmother. Seeking a positive loving relationship of normalcy, Angi was manipulated to move in with her father and stepmother only to find out the motive was cessation of child support payments and a deep hatred that was exhibited in every manner possible.

During the next four years, Angi underwent terrible mental abuse by the hands of her stepmother and a father who chose to turn his head rather than protect her. The first Christmas at her father's home, she awoke to find that they had gone to her stepmother's family's home, taking all the Christmas presents. Angi awoke to find an empty house, no explanation telling her where they were, and no invitation for her to join them. She soon developed a dread of every holiday because she knew she would be left alone and uncared for.

Angi's relationship with her younger sister created a parental nature inside Angi. Angi recalls making sure her sister ate lunch, scrounging up fifty cents to buy little pizzas sold at the local Village Pantry that Angi would heat up in their microwave. Often, she would be hungry but only have enough money to buy food for her sister. Angi recalls taking her sister to a downtown store the day before her first day of kindergarten having saved her babysitting money to buy her a new outfit to wear on the first day. Angi still treasures a photograph she took of her sister the morning of her first day of school, somehow holding the maturity to know the importance of recording this important day.

During high school, Angi worked and saved her money to move out of her father's home the day after graduation at the age of seventeen years old. The ten year age difference meant her sister was only seven years old and Angi's absence would expose her younger sister to a horrific abusive life. To this day, Angi regrets leaving her little sister and wishes she could have understood the potential risks her sister would face once Angi moved out.

Often when teenagers do not feel loved and cared for they look to fill these voids in other ways. In a lot of cases the other way is not healthy. They try loveless sex without the understanding that this is not love. Girls will then have a baby thinking that they finally have someone who will love them unconditionally. Drugs or alcohol are often used for numbing the pain.

Angi acknowledges the fact that she did not resort to any of these dysfunctional behaviors as a result of her abusive childhood. She acknowledges also that getting employment at a local hospital created a form of family for her. She had coworkers who cared about her and provided her long-term positive relationships. She did get married at the young age of eighteen and had her first child at the age of twenty-one.

Besides having the support of her coworkers in the hospital, Angi felt supported by her stepfather Michael Johnson. He married Angi's mother when Angi was fifteen but it was an off and on marriage, mostly off. He met his current wife in 2002 and eventually married her. Angi expected rejection from his new wife, Laura. She thought that a stepdaughter from another

marriage would be looked at as an unwanted intrusion. That never happened and Laura always accepted Angi.

At age twenty-one, Angi started college at Ball State University in Muncie, Indiana. She was a non-traditional student who was married and the mother of a three-year-old child.

Although she did not want to become a nurse, she did not know what she did want to do. She followed her family tradition of nursing and chose it as her profession because she recognized the job security of working in the health field. She was in the highly competitive Associate RN program. Angi learned that she held the key to changing her destiny in life. She worked hard, and utilized her resources and intelligence as a method of continuous improvement and learning. While in college she learned that people who do not feel loved seek out love in other ways. She considered herself fortunate that she found what appeared to be constructive ways to find love and live her life.

While working as a Registered Nurse in the Intensive Care Unit, Angi vividly recalls having a serious traumatic brain injury patient. He was only a fifth grader who suffered from a self-inflicted gunshot wound to the front of his brain while looking at his father's gun. An accidental discharge, the gun had previously been locked, being only out of safety after a recent home break-in. She recalled this particular case had always stayed with her and the patient did recover after a lengthy unstable period where a neurosurgeon worked nonstop to stabilize and keep this little boy alive. Little did she know, this case turned out to be serendipitous as years later this doctor would actually save her life.

Angi had a never ending drive to better herself. She earned her second college degree in advanced business. **During this period, state and federal healthcare plans were privatizing their Medicaid and Medicare programs after the states found themselves inadequate in effectively administering health plans**

and funding. Angi was instrumental in launching several private Medicaid plans and then Medicare. She worked for the largest health plan in the world, finding herself advancing up the chain to executive leadership positions. She developed the regulatory, compliance auditing program, oversaw multi-million dollar projects, and became a subject matter expert in the areas of data driven statistics. She was promoted working for the Medicare program over New York and
Connecticut. This position found her working sixty to seventy hours a week, traveling out of state every couple of weeks.

As some marriages go by the wayside when the couple is young and inexperienced, Angi's marriage did not last. Acknowledging that people change as they age and the fact that her background never prepared her for how to effectively have a solid marriage, at no fault of her or her ex-husband, they parted and got divorced. **She had memories of learning what she did not want but, through no fault of her own, she had no memories to learn what she did want and how to have a stable marriage.**

Surprisingly, her story ill prepared her for 2009, where she experienced the top four major life stressors all at the same time. She was going through a divorce, she changed jobs, she was moving and worst of all, her twenty-nine-year-old sister suddenly passed away. Since the age of seventeen, her sister had struggled with coping as an adult and turned to drugs and alcohol as a resort. Angi never fully realized the depth of her sister's struggles until it was too late.

Angi's sister had pancreatitis and blood hemorrhaging which caused clotting factors. Eventually the blood filled her lungs and she died. Angi struggled with guilt from abandoning her and not protecting her from abusive adults. "My sister always told me I was the strong one. That she wasn't as strong as me."

Around this time, Angi began dating her now husband Troy and blended their families. He had three sons and she had two daughters.

Frank Healy

It was similar to *The Brady Bunch*. Troy and Angi determined to give their children all the attention and love that Angi did not get as a child. She notes, **"It was vital that our children never felt they were treated differently. I recall my half-sister having a dream bedroom at the age of four. You know, the bed with the fabric canopy. All while our rooms only had a mattress on the floor."**

During this time, Angi began experiencing bouts of bacterial infections. She notes for the next year, she was on antibiotics at least thirteen or fourteen times for a variety of infections. At the time, she contributed this to the stress and recent experiences. Next, she began exhibiting fogginess, extreme lethargy, her hair fell out, and she developed circular psoriasis ulcerations on her body.

After a couple of years in her new marriage, Angi began getting headaches. This began a long ordeal of seeing doctor after doctor. In this age of specialists, every doctor seemed to tell her something different. Her adrenal glands were not working, Retinal Edema, Hypertension, the list goes on. It got to where she was bedridden most of the time and had given up hope. However, her husband encouraged her to keep looking and she did not want to subject him or the children to her death.

Finally, she sought out the neurosurgeon she recalled helping during that case with the fifth grader many years prior. During this time, the fragmentation in her healthcare providers and specialists left her in an almost hopeless state of accepting she was going to die. Her husband told her this will be the final doctor. Mustering up the courage to expose herself to yet another healthcare provider after numerous misdiagnosis, undiagnosis, and unethical care, she agreed. "I told myself, I'm going to die after this. I was preparing myself and was discussing with Troy what our plans would be with the kids, and so on."

Her visit with that neurosurgeon revealed that if there was a medical problem with her brain, it would show up in testing. He ordered a test called an MRV, which is like an MRI, but it tests the veins of the brain. Waiting on the results, she underwent a lumbar puncture test under anesthesia so they could get a true reading of the pressure in her brain and determine if it was elevated. "That morning, they almost did not take me to get this puncture test because my blood pressure was one hundred and seventy over one hundred and forty-five." Even after administering several blood pressure medications, she was informed they would not perform this test if her blood pressure did not decrease to a safer measurement. Luckily, her blood pressure lowered and they were able to perform the test, but in post-op, she awoke to concerned faces from the medical staff. "I knew it was bad. I asked the neurosurgeon what my pressure reading was and he told me it was thirty-six. The pressure in my head was higher than the gunshot-wound-to-the-head case I used to care for."

The MRV test revealed the veins located on the left side of her brain did not work or drain. Her brain pressure needed to be around eleven and they informed her that the veins could not be repaired. The damaged veins were a result of the multiple head injuries she sustained as a child at the hands of her father. The neurosurgeon placed an atrial portal shunt into the middle of her brain. This shunt is magnetized to control her brain pressure so that it stays around a measurement of eleven like it should be.

Before consulting the neurosurgeon Dr. Sylvania, Angi had spent the last five years consulting doctors. Unfortunately all of the specialists she saw seemed to have their own agenda. She began spending time in bed and at one point lost all hope. Her supportive husband Troy and her children gave her a reason to go on living. Eventually her condition required surgery. She is now recovered and her enthusiasm for life has returned.

Over the years, Angi has learned many life lessons from her traumatic memories. She learned that bad times end and you can persevere. She learned that you hold the keys to your journey. This belief helped her heal her guilt over her sister's death. She realizes she did what she could and everyone makes their own decisions. After her sister's death her mother and father reunited. Angi's father divorced her stepmother in 2010. Angi thought the reconciliation was a bad idea. After just two weeks her father broke her mother's arm in a fight and it seemed like the same thing over again. Angi learned that you can't make people do what you think is the best thing. They make their own decisions and you can only control your journey and how those around you will impact it.

Angi tells of a soul searching experience at this time in her life. Comparing herself to an ATM machine, she relates that each relationship may deposit or add to your life and at times, debit or take away. But there are those dysfunctional individuals that when you examine how they impact your life, they only debit or take away without ever depositing or adding. She decided to remove those individuals who were not enriching her and no longer offers others the opportunity to take away anything from her life anymore.

Perhaps surprisingly, Angi's stepfather Michael continues to be one of the metaphorical machines that add to her life. When they are together, he introduces her as his daughter and he always counts her among his kids. He even refers to her children as his grandchildren. Angi learned from this that life gave her this lesson of how not to trust those who are closest to you, your family, who should be trusted no matter what. Life flipped her over and said, "Let me show you that you will be blessed with those around you who love you even more than a parent ever could and they will not be connected to you in such a way that it is a given."

Have you ever noticed how some people make you feel happy when you are around them and you become energetic? Hopefully your friends are like that to you. Then there are those people who drain you and you feel tired and annoyed while you are around them and wish they would go away? I call those people emotional vampires. They can potentially have long-term negative impacts over a lifetime. Angi has used this metaphor as a reminder to stay away from toxic people.

Reflecting back on all of her experiences, she notes she wouldn't change a thing, except for her sister. Each of those experiences created the strong woman you see today. "I had created a successful coping method as a result of my abusive childhood that left me with a steel cage around my heart. All of a sudden, my illness took away my ability to self-survive and I had to rely and trust Troy that he would stick beside me through thick and thin. I feel my purpose was to only know a lack of love and trust while growing up, to as an adult, having to rely one hundred percent on the love and trust of others when I could no longer take care of myself."

Angi is currently writing a book about the fragmentation she experienced with our current healthcare system in hopes of eliminating this risk for others in the future. You can visit her website at www.AskaNurseNow.info.

Angi found her calling through a combination of good and bad life events. Our next story is about a man whose horrific memory in young adulthood totally changed the direction of his life.

Chapter 9

Find Your Calling Through A Horrific Memory: The Story of a Victim Turned "Expert"

Dean Tong was estranged from his wife. What could be worse than a failed marriage with a small child? In 1985, Dean was at work as a laboratory medical technologist when he got a call from his attorney who represented him in the custody case for their three-year-old daughter. His wife had accused him of sexual abuse towards their daughter. Shortly after the call, **Tong with his attorney by his side turned himself in to the authorities**. Dean spent two weeks in jail and faced a long ordeal of expensive and emotionally taxing legal battles. He was charged with capital sexual battery and was not allowed to see his children **for well over a year**.

"It seemed surreal. It was as if a lightning bolt came out of the sky and struck me," stated Dean. The hardest part was losing visitation of his children.

The jail sentence was followed by fourteen months of court hearings before the district attorney's office decided not to file charges due to a lack of evidence. The state knew they would not be able to obtain a conviction beyond a reasonable doubt. **He spent ten years and over one hundred thousand dollars in court to clear his name.** He sued for damages and visitation rights. He describes the whole long episode as a "Fatherectomy."

It would have been easy for Dean to become depressed and think of himself as a victim. However, he decided to turn his nightmare into a force, a weapon for fathers who are falsely accused of abuse. He started speaking publicly about false allegations. Soon he became well known - **a**
published author, a candidate for Florida politics, and an activist. He started a consulting office for parents and attorneys called Abuse Excuse. He has given expert testimony to courts in fourteen states and served parents accused of abuse and their attorneys in cases from all fifty states.

Dean's resume is incredibly impressive. He has published three books, commentated in many famous cases, and he has been on over two thousand radio shows and the guest on national television talk shows.

In 1992, when he was still in court to clear his name, he wrote his first book, *Don't Blame ME, Daddy, False Accusations of Child Sexual Abuse*. He wrote this book to prove his innocence and it helped him. Encouraged by this, he wrote *Ashes To Ashes, Families to Dust* which has information for the falsely accused. This was followed in 2002 with *Elusive Innocence, A Survival Guide for the Falsely Accused*.
He wrote this book to help attorneys understand the dynamics of false abuse cases. **That book is in its fifth printing.**

Additionally, Dean had speaking engagements. In 2000, he spoke at the Father's Day Rally in Washington D.C. The rally was to raise awareness for fathers who were not allowed to participate in the rearing of their children due to exaggerated or mistaken abuse claims.

By this time, Dean was well known and his services were sought in every state. He was on the legal team for the Darren Mack case. Darren was charged with the murder of his exwife and for sniper shooting his divorce judge. In 2003 through 2005, he aligned with

Court-TV for the sexual child abuse allegations against Michael Jackson. In 2004 he was a media commentator on MSNBC in the Kobe Bryant sexual assault case, and was a guest on *Dr. Phil* where the topic was mothers accused of coaching their children to accuse their fathers of sexual assault. He also appeared on *The Montel Williams Show* and CNN's *Nancy Grace*. Dean was also a media consultant on WFTV Channel 9 during the trial of Casey Anthony, the Elian González affair, and the murder of John Benet Ramsey.

Legislation protecting children has been influenced by Dean. He worked with former Senator Jim Hargrett of the Florida Legislature to pass the Child Spanking Bill by helping him word it and define the limits of abuse. He also helped in the passage of the Malicious False Abuse Law which aims to protect those falsely accused, and he helped in the repeal of the Florida Child Abuse Registry.

Dean's thirst for knowledge led him to the United Kingdom in 2000, and in 2006, he received a Master of Science Degree in Psychology and The Law in Child Forensic Studies at the University of Portsmouth and Leeds. His master's thesis was published in the *Journal of American Family Therapy* in 2007. It was entitled, *The Penile Plethysmograph, Abel Assessment For Sexual Interest and MSI-II: Are They Speaking The Same Language?*

Today Dean continues his ascension up the expert ladder as a public speaker, author, consultant and trial expert. Recently, he became a diplomat to the American Board of Forensic Examiners (www.acfei.org). He is a living example of how you can turn an unhappy and trying memory into a lifetime commitment and calling. When I asked Dean what keeps him going he said that pictures of kids from his court cases give him "Fire in the belly." Ironically, that's the same title of a book authored by Sam Keen.

The Ultimate Guide To Healing Your Past

For more information on Dean and his services you can visit his website Abuse Excuse, Dean Tong Consultancy at http://abuse-excuse.com.

While nobody would want to be falsely accused of a crime, especially of hurting their own child, Dean made the most of it. Our next story is about a man who overcame a family tragedy that no one would want to happen.

Chapter 10

A Club That No One Wants to Join – Survivors Of Family Suicide

It has now been almost fifty years since Carl David, a successful writer and art dealer in Philadelphia, Pennsylvania, had a family tragedy. When Carl was sixteen years old his big brother committed suicide.

After the tragedy, every day seemed long. Each sunrise just meant that it was another day without his brother. After his brother's death, Carl and his family followed their Jewish tradition of sitting shiva. This means that for a week everyone in the immediate and extended family stays together to support each other and to honor the deceased relative.

The most challenging time after a loss is not immediately after the death. At that time everyone is there for support. After the extended family leaves, the immediate family needs to support each other.

Carl's parents went to therapy after sitting shiva ended. They needed to deal with the guilt and to continue nurturing the two children that they were still raising. They felt that they lost their will to live. The whole family did their best to support each other and tried not create any undue stress.

Carl continued to go to school and after graduation went to Temple University in Philadelphia. However, he was expelled after two years and found a college in Georgia, Oglethorpe College named after the governor of Georgia when it was a penal colony in colonial times. He graduated from Oglethorpe.

During these years, Carl disassociated himself from the experience of losing his brother. Every time the thought of the death came into his head he blocked it. However, he realized he could not block it out forever, and his brother was still in his thoughts. He went to therapy for four years. The therapist encouraged him to write about the experience and he wrote his now published book *Bader Field, How My Family Survived Suicide.*

When a loved one commits suicide, there are typical thoughts and feelings that people go through. For a long time Carl wrestled with the question, why did his brother not share his feelings and ask for help? He did not realize that people who really want to end their lives don't share their thoughts and feelings, they just do it and do not want anyone stopping them. People who issue a cry for help often do not want to succeed – they want someone to know how much pain they are in and to help them.

Carl also blamed himself because he did not notice any signs that his brother was suicidal. He resolved this by understanding that there were no signs.

Despite the obvious fact that you can't know for sure what a person who commits suicide was thinking, the conclusions you draw from what you knew of the person can be useful in healing the memory. Carl now concludes that if his brother had shared how he was feeling he would still be alive. Carl has forgiven his brother for that. He has also forgiven himself for not noticing signs since there were no signs.

Carl also believes that if his brother had known how much pain his suicide would cause his family he would not have done it. When people are suicidal they get into a bubble that no one can penetrate and they can't see or get out of it. Consequently they can't think of the pain that their actions would cause to others. They are too self-absorbed.

Some people might think of it as odd for someone to say that their relationship with a dead person improved. However, with all of the feelings that people go through after a loss you really do still have a relationship with the person who passed away. It seems that Carl's relationship with his brother improved after Carl healed himself. The worst thing that you can say to a bereaved person is, "Get over it" – they will always feel a connection to their lost loved one. People often stay sad for a long time because they believe that the sadness is the only connection they still have. I tell my clients that they can still feel connected by remembering the good times. When they can do that more than feel sad they have healed.

Carl describes the period after he healed as being "On a mission." The experience of writing the book *Bader Field, How My Family Survived Suicide* was painful yet cathartic. Bader Field in Atlantic City, New Jersey, was the last place that he saw his father alive. He decided to make educating people about suicide and helping the bereaved families part of his life's work. Since 2008, he has advocated for bereaved families on radio and television.

Additionally, Carl learned from the experience that children, even adult children need to know that they are loved. He has always made sure his own children know this. In his own words, "I did not tell my kids until they were old enough to not freak out." He helped them see the degree of collateral destruction that a suicide can cause. "Suicide is a permanent solution to a temporary problem," is the way he views it.

To learn more about Carl and his works go to the following websites:

The Ultimate Guide To Healing Your Past

☐   www.carledavid.com, ☐
www.daviddavidgallery.com, ☐
www.askart.com/DDavid.

Chapter 11

This Is No M*A*S*H, This Is Real War

No one had ever had to tell Sarah Blum what to do with her life. This young girl from Atlantic City, New Jersey, always felt that she was being guided in certain directions. In elementary school, she created a career booklet and felt drawn to nursing. At first she wanted to be a doctor. Her uncle was an attorney and said he would put her through medical school, but unfortunately her uncle died in her sophomore year in high school. Since there seemed to be no possibility of funding for medical school, she instead went to Albert Einstein Medical Center in Philadelphia and studied nursing. While she was in nursing school she declared to her fellow students, "If there is a war and I am still single, I will go."

At age twenty-three, she went to Los Angeles, California, and worked as a nurse. Tensions were growing in Vietnam by 1966 and when the opportunity came for her to go there, she went.

Before going to Vietnam, she worked at Letterman Army Hospital in the San Francisco area. In order to get to her unit she had to walk past a corridor of maimed veterans. They wore royal blue pajamas and had blank and piercing stares even when she was one hundred yards away. Despite the piercing stares, she found that she could not stand to just walk past such needy men and began talking to them as she made her way to her unit.

Sarah recalls one man with red hair and blue eyes. He had lost both legs in the war when a nine-year-old kid threw a hand grenade at the truck he was in. The man had plans to be the best man at his friend's wedding that December and he asked Sarah to bring him to the wedding to help him stand on his prosthetic legs. She went and did help him stand for five minutes. He could not sit down again fast enough.

Shortly after the wedding she flew to Vietnam for active duty. Being new to the system she did not know what she was getting into. She agreed to an assignment in the Twelfth Evacuation Hospital. She met another nurse who had just been given another assignment out of there because the working conditions were so bad. She told Sarah to get out if she could.

Sarah discovered that she was in the busiest area in all of Vietnam. It was a constant flow of casualties and body bags. Her duties included opening the wounds of her patients, removing any shrapnel and dead tissue inside, irrigating the wound with saline solution, and then applying a bandage. Other nurses on the wards would flush out and re bandage the wound every four hours for three days and three nights. After those three days and night, they would come back to the operating room for a delayed primary closure, or a DPC.

When you think of the cleanliness and security protection of today's civilian hospitals it is hard to imagine the deplorable conditions in Vietnam. Grenades and mortars flew by as Sarah worked on the wounded. They trained her to focus on her work and to block out the danger. She did the best she could but always lived in fear while helping the surgeons.

Not only were the adults killing and maiming each other, but the Viet Cong taught their children to threaten Americans. One time a little boy handed her a Coke with formaldehyde and ground glass in it. The idea was that it would kill her if she was

thirsty and desperate enough to drink it. Another time a little girl pulled a gun on her. This was similar to the nine-year-old kid who had thrown a grenade at the truck which maimed the soldier at Letterman.

One day they brought in a man who had been hit by American artillery. His legs had been obliterated and were hanging by skin and his pelvis had also been horribly mutilated. Everyone looked at each other with puzzlement – nobody knew what to do. They amputated his legs to the hip and there was little left of him below his pelvis. Sarah stood in his blood for hours.

Two days later she arrived early before the other staff. She walked towards the man's stretcher. The stretcher was flat from the foot-end up to the bump in the middle and her eyes followed up from the bump to his chest and his face.

At this point, something snapped in Sarah. She tried to talk but at first nothing would come out. She ran out of the door and yelled, "Kill, kill, kill! That's all you know. I have got to get out of here." They gave her a three day break where she laid on a beach, cried, and prayed. She visualized a wall around her heart. When she returned to duty she had numbed herself sufficiently to continue her duties. In the 1960s there was not much knowledge of Posttraumatic Stress Disorder (PTSD). This is extreme stress cause by traumatic events.

Sarah eventually returned to the U.S. but continued to work with the wounded. When her plane landed they kept everybody on until protestors were quelled.

Back in the United States, Sarah was assigned as the head nurse in an orthopedic ward at Madigan Army Hospital in Washington State. With less pressure around her she noticed that many of the men with wounds were not healing properly. It seemed that they had emotional wounds which needed to be addressed in order for their physical bodies to heal. At that time the medical profession did not accept that there was a mind-body connection. However, the doctor noticed that Sarah was a good listener and supported her working with the wounded that needed counseling. She discovered that when she opened her heart and listened to them it helped them heal.

Sarah decided to go to school for psychotherapy because she liked counseling the wounded soldiers. She got her bachelor's degree and worked with veterans. Then from 1974 to 1976, she went to graduate school for psychosocial nursing.

On Tuesday, April 29, 1975, Sarah sat in her graduate class when she heard the news that Saigon fell. She felt that everything our country had done over there was completely undone. She left class and walked around in a daze. She went and talked to her advisor but the advisor knew nothing about Posttraumatic Stress Disorder. She felt she had to thicken the wall that she built around her heart on the beach eight years earlier.

In January of 1981, Sarah heard that the hostages from Iran were being released. They played the song "Tie A Yellow Ribbon Round The Old Oak Tree." She became angry that they were given a hero's welcome when the Vietnam veterans had been treated so poorly.

Around that time she saw an article for support of women who were in Vietnam. The therapist was starting her own group for women Vietnam veterans in Seattle so Sarah went there for therapy for her PTSD. The therapist created a safe environment. That group was only the beginning. She found another therapist and dealt with issues that included a fear of her own explosiveness. It could destroy everything in its path. She pounded a pillow and yelled and screamed at the injustices of the war. She yelled at the impact of the war and how wrong it was. When she finished she saw that the others in the room were not breathing. Eventually they took deep breaths and their color returned. She let out a sigh and knew that the wall was down.

Sarah learned many life lessons from her memories of Vietnam and working with wounded soldiers. She developed a stronger sense of self than she ever had. She developed a greater capacity for love, compassion, and expressing herself. All of these tools have helped her in her career. Now she continues to see all kinds of clients with PTSD. Sarah is the author of the book *Women Under Fire, Abuse In The Military*. You can learn more about Sarah and her book on her website at http://womenunderfire.net.

While Sarah saw many of the soldiers who gave their lives and their health for freedom and the great American Dream, our next story shows that sometimes the American Dream can backfire.

Chapter 12

The American Dream Of Land Ownership Gone Sour

You may remember all the quotes and phrases from history class about the American Dream such as "Forty acres and a mule," or, "America, the land of opportunity." The Homestead Act of 1862 offered average citizens the opportunity to claim up to one hundred and sixty acres of land from the government and develop it. Long gone in 2016, it gave many people a chance to work hard, save money, and truly get a piece of the American Dream.

One of my favorite movie endings is in the 1992 film *Far and Away* with Tom Cruise and Nicole Kidman. The actors play Irish immigrants who come to America after a fight with their landlord. Over many months they face hardships involving work and money. Shannon, the landlord's daughter (played by Kidman) takes various jobs such as being a nightclub dancer. Joseph (Tom Cruise) enters boxing competitions but when he loses one match their money is stolen. They go through the winter destitute. The next summer Joseph is reminded in a dream about his desire for land ownership. They hurry to Oklahoma to participate in a Homestead Act-inspired race for land. The last scene in the movie is Joseph proudly and happily staking the flag on his new property. The audience feels delighted for them as they begin their new life after accomplishing their dream.

Movies are one thing, reality is another. In the mid1990s, Bill Seavey and his wife, Laurel, were searching for the ultimate

rural property to buy and develop. They traveled throughout the west and were self-avowed experts on living in small towns. This couple had started the twoperson Greener Pastures Institute (GPI) which had garnered much media attention beginning around 1989.

In 1994, they read about some lots for sale at a one thousand acre subdivision called Ponderosa Village located in eastern Washington State. Bill knew the developer from his business dealings involving GPI and the developer's original homestead lot of five acres was offered to them for a reasonable price. Ponderosa Village was founded as an ecological community of diverse housing approaches such as log cabins and geodesic domes as well as more conventional structures.

The property was only three miles to a small town, had a breathtaking view of Mt. Hood, a well, and was partially forested. The Seaveys planned to park their RV there for the summer, build storage sheds, and apply for permits to build a mortgage-free straw bale house. They went to an on-site workshop on the building technique and were encouraged that their twenty-five thousand dollars in cash might allow them to get a home built with volunteers they planned to recruit from several states.

During this time, they enjoyed watching animals cross the land, they met their new neighbors – many handy selfsufficient types attracted to the community – and they began the process of applying for a building permit aided by a Seattle architect who had experience in the method of building straw bale homes.

As the long hot summer of 1995 wore on, the politics at Ponderosa Village began to heat up. One man started a dispute over the ownership of the well. His accusation was that the owners were making it difficult for the well to be accessible to the people who needed it. Seavey's well was actually on an easement shared by others in the community. Washington State was beginning to put pressure on land owners who had only trailers with no septic tanks installed.

Within this period of time, it turned out that the Seaveys' straw bale building project was the very first to hit the permitting stream in Klickitat County, a region where forest products such as lumber were king. **Several thousand dollars later, a storage building had been erected, a septic system installed, electricity was established at the lot line, and architectural renderings were completed. Then the local building official refused to issue a permit, except to build and pour a foundation, and bumped up the plans to the International Conference of Building Officials (ICBO) in Seattle which insisted on testing for fire safety even though straw bale walls, being thick and coated with concrete stucco, are probably among the most fire-resistant buildings in the world. This refusal would require the barn-raising workshop to be cancelled and delay the project by at least a year.**

The Seaveys didn't have the funds to wait it out or to appeal the decision. Over the next few months, Bill wrote letters to officials in the government and the ICBO but to no avail. They contacted Pacific Legal Foundation, a public interest legal group, but they claimed they couldn't help due to limited funding. Part of the whole story was told in an issue of *Fine Homebuilding*.

Bill told his wife, who was born with Spinal Bifida, a partially disabling disease that had hampered her throughout her life, that he felt he had failed her. He told her that if she still wanted to be together she would need to make a choice to either stay in Washington or Oregon with his support, or move to Baja California, Mexico, where he owned a lot in a resort and they could start building there. She chose Mexico and for three months they licked their wounds living out of their small motor home. They got approvals quickly and poured a foundation for a straw bale house, but by spring they had run out of money and

Frank Healy

a publisher of one of Seavey's books was insisting they return to the states or his contract would be cancelled.

They moved into a youth hostel for several months along the central California coast where Bill assisted the owner with chores. Laurel was not happy and they were essentially broke with few immediate prospects for income. Their relationship, based on love and trust, had begun to fray and Bill suggested they separate indefinitely, with Laurel returning home to Michigan possibly to live with her parents.

Over the next few months, Bill resided in a small office where he worked to save money on rent. Laurel moved back home with her family but it wasn't working out. She wanted her car back and for Bill to drive it to her. He said he would, but then he changed his mind. (He had previously shipped her cat back.) This started months of nasty phone calls and emails.

At one point, Laurel decided to sell the Ponderosa property out of desperation. Bill had made sure when they purchased the property that it was in her name. A Village co-founder bought it for about one thousand dollars, significantly less then what they paid or what it was worth. Bill was surprised and tried to convince Laurel to persuade the co-founder to return the property if a repurchase price could be arranged, but it was to no avail.

Laurel was admitted to a psychiatric facility in Maine after she had attempted suicide following an effort to reconcile with her previous husband who lived in the east. By this time Bill had begun dating another woman, whom he eventually married. At one point, he had to make a wrenching decision whether to stay with his future wife, or to reunite with Laurel, whom he of course still loved.

Meanwhile, Laurel was discharged from the hospital, but did not follow through with counseling or medication and went back to living with a friend. She could not get Social Security Income at one point because of legally being a property owner – a factor in her

69

decision to sell the Ponderosa property. With the one thousand dollars she received from the sale of the property, she decided to go back to California, reclaim her car which Bill agreed to give her, and go from there.

Staying with friends in the Los Angeles area, she one day must have become extremely despondent and walked in front of a train. Bill and his girlfriend got a phone call in the middle of the night and rushed to the hospital which was two hundred miles way. It was too late. Laurel was pronounced brain dead. A service was held for her locally and was attended by her friends, Bill's kin, and Laurel's prior husband, but none of her immediate relatives.

Bill struggled with guilt for a long time and believed he could have saved her somehow. It also took him a very long time to recover from his anger over the Ponderosa land fiasco. Writing the small self-published book *Greener Pastures* helped him heal somewhat.

Bill married Eleanor three weeks after Laurel's death. It took him many years to come to terms with what happened and to partially forgive himself. It was an extraordinary set of circumstances that led to the tragedy, but tragedies are often a part of life – and few are spared.

Bill's path in the past twenty years has been one of charitable pursuits particularly with the homeless, publishing inspirational self-help books (see www.williamseavey.com), trying to be a devoted husband to Eleanor, and a supportive granddad. The Seaveys run a successful small bed and breakfast together and life is good. But he takes little for granted about what the future may hold.

You have now taken a journey through all kinds of adventures. Perhaps you felt sad as you read the stories but happy for the people as they triumphed and overcame

adversities. The purpose of these stories was not to upset you but to inspire you.

Some people actually enjoy watching the news because they unwittingly practice the Social Comparison Theory. The idea of this theory is that they compare themselves favorably to the people whose houses burned down or who were in a shootout. While this seems callous and even sadistic it does help people feel better. Often when a child is abducted parents who hear about it immediately think that the parents did not protect the child. If I were a parent of the abducted child I certainly would not want any of those news viewers near me. The idea is that the parents who heard about it want to believe that if they protect their child well enough the child will be safe.

Other people enjoy hearing stories like this because it shows the human spirit as dauntless. When you hear of others overcoming adversity you believe that you can do the same. However, some of you might think, yes, but my problems are not nearly as intense as these people's, my story is quite boring. In the next chapter you will learn that it does not matter what you have been through. Even everyday unpleasant memories should be healed and learned from.

Chapter 13

My Memories Were Not That Dramatic, But They Still Haunt Me

After hearing all of those dramatic stories, you may think that you do not have a right to be upset about your own past. I hear this frequently from my clients in my Anxiety and Depression Management Groups. First they share how good their life looks on the outside. For example, I might have a young lady who has a good job, two wonderful children, and a wonderful husband. She can't understand why she feels depressed or anxious. Usually she feels this way because she needs to heal her past.

Many of the clients whom I coach and counsel do not have as much drama in their lives as the people whose stories you read, but they still need to heal. This is because five people can have five different reactions to the same event. For example, one person is raised in an alcoholic environment where there is physical and verbal abuse. He decides to involve himself in school and community activities to limit his time in the house. He learns the value of hard work through sports and music and learns to care for others through church activities. He looks to his coaches and his friends' parents as role models and learns good values from them. Meanwhile, someone else in a similar environment takes to the streets, gets involved with drugs, violence, loveless sex. He spends his adult life in and out of jail, rehabs, and dies at forty.

While both men's lives sound dramatic, the first one chose a productive life over a dramatic life. The second one did what he knew and never learned anything better.

Then there is the child who cries when they see starving people on television. They get teased by other kids because they react so strongly. When they get older they volunteer for the Peace Corps and take a career as a teacher or a counselor. However, they still have to heal their memories from being picked on and teased when they were young.

Sometimes young people are subject to subtle abuse from their parents at home. Their parents might yell at them or criticize them on purpose to toughen them for the big bad world otherwise they will not make it in life. At least that is what the parents believe. These memories may not be very dramatic but the person still needs to heal.

Studies have shown that a portion of the population is highly sensitive. This means that they feel things more intensely than others. They get upset over verbal banter, hot days, cold days, dark rooms, seeing people hurt and anything else that affects people emotionally. It does not mean that they have twenty-twenty vision or exceptionally good hearing, it just means that they feel things more strongly and deeply than other people who aren't highly sensitive.

Since we all tend to remember things that have emotional significance, sensitive people may have more to heal than others. **If you think you are a highly sensitive person, chin up, there are advantages. You may feel pain and hurt more strongly than others, but you also enjoy things more easily and need less stimulation to be satisfied.** Imagine a group of kids sitting at a mall. The sensitive one would be content to sit there all day and chat. The less sensitive kids would get bored quickly and want to get in their separate cars, chase each other around the parking lot at one hundred miles per hour and throw beer bottles from the car. (Please note that this example is hypothetical, I do not want to be sued if someone's seventeen-year-old kid did this.) The sensitive kid gets nauseas at the thought of something like this.

If you are a sensitive person, don't think that it is wrong or silly to heal memories that are not that dramatic. Essentially you are the one who decides what needs healing. The only rule is that if you get bothered, annoyed, anxious, panicky, or angry about a past memory, then you need to heal it and learn from it. You are the expert.

Frank Healy

Chapter 14

You Are the Smartest Person in the World

What do you mean I am the smartest person in the world?
I am not an expert at anything. I was average in school, I'm average at work, and I'm average at home. What do you mean?

I mean that we are all experts in what we need to know. All of your memories happened to teach you something. Your past relationships taught you what you want, don't want, or some of what you want. The same thing happened with your past jobs, friends, everything.

Many times people repeat similar scenarios in their lives because they do not learn the lesson the first, second, or even third time so life keeps attempting to teach them. For example, if you keep making friends with people who humiliate you or guilt trip you, it may be time to set limits with people. When you become confident that you can set limits with people and make them respect you then you will present in a way that bully types will not want to be around you. The opposite of that is that people who respect you *will* want to be around you.

Life is arranged so that everyone gets the opportunity to learn what they need to learn. Maybe you have had a hard time making money your whole life and someone else made their first million before they were thirty. Maybe knowing this will teach you to budget money better and to enjoy life and be grateful for

what you have. The millionaire in turn may need to learn to give some money to charity and not spend it all on pleasures. It is all what we need.

In addition to learning life lessons, it is always good to learn new things independent of school. Some people never read a book after they finish their formal schooling while others keep taking classes or learning through their own efforts for a lifetime. Have you ever heard of Lifetime Learning? Usually this applies to educational media and the Learning Library. However, Lifetime Learning is a good slogan for anyone.

Most people who choose to learn something independent of work or school requirements choose something that appeals to them. It makes sense to learn more about something that you have a natural interest in. Professionals and tradespeople always want to learn more about their niche career. If you have a hobby or specific interest in something not associated with your day job, you can keep learning about that, too.

Some people seem to have a natural tendency to learn from their memories. When something does not work they won't try the same way again. All small children learn that when they put the palm of their hand on the hot stove it burns so they never do it again. For some people, this general concept spills into their everyday life. For example, when they play baseball, if the way they swing the bat does not get them a hit, they will adjust their swing. If a certain way to socialize does not work they try another way. These people are the ones who grow up to be well adjusted adults.

Then there are other people who keep making the same mistakes and have memories of failure. These people do not use their memories to learn to do things differently. There is the old expression, "Insanity is doing the same thing over and over and expecting different results." I don't know about you but I do not like being around people who think they already know everything and are unwilling to learn anything new.

People who do not want to learn new things come in many forms. Besides the know-it-all form, they can be self-proclaimed victims. "Why does everything happen to me?" This victim mentality could be overcome if they were willing to learn from their mistakes. Then there are the people who are socially inflexible and treat everyone the same. This could be a good thing if their one way to treat everyone is with high regard. This would not be such a good thing though if you happen to be their boss and you don't want to be talked to like a teenager yo!

I hope that reading this book has made you aware that to be intelligent, happy, and successful you need to keep learning from your memories. Every time something does not go your way it is an opportunity to adjust, and when things go your way it is an opportunity to learn how to keep your life moving in the right direction.

Afterword

I hope you have enjoyed reading The Ultimate Self Help Guide To Healing Your Past. Whether you were inspired by the stories, intrigued by the personal sharing, or benefitted from the exercises, you have been on an exciting journey of self-exploration. This is a journey that you can continue to take throughout your life. With each passing day you can learn something from every experience you have and every memory that surfaces.

I am planning a course on Udemy which can take you further in your learnings. I also have a free report **http://www.phenomenalmemory.com/products/** and here are the links to my other books.

Heal Your Memories, Change Your Life

http://www.amazon.com/Heal-Memories-ChangeRevised-Edition-ebook/dp/B00RRD7UJ2

Memory Quiz, What Type Of Learner Are You?

http://www.amazon.es/Memory-Learner-Phenomenal-English-Edition-ebook/dp/B007VUL4U2

Contributors

I would like to express my deepest thanks to ....

Kelly Meister for contributing and helping me see the various modalities that can be used to heal the past. Here is Kelly's website www.crazycritterlady.com.

Richard London for you interview. I enjoy reading you're a Handbook For Life newsletter each month. Here is Richard's website. www.AHandbookForLife.com

Amy Sherman, thank you for interviewing and showing us that visualizations and right actions really do work. You can access Amy's website at amybethsherman@gmail.com. You can get information on her organization Baby Boomers Network at www.yourbabyboomersnetwork.com

Angi McElfresh, Thank you for sharing your story which is inspirational on many levels. To see and order Angi's's book and products go to www.AskaNurseNow.info.

Dean Tong, thank you for taking the time to contribute. The work you do throughout the world to help the falsely accused is phenomenal. Here is Dean's website at http://abuseexcuse.com

Carl David, thank you for sharing your poignant story and what you learned. Here are Carl's websites www.carledavid.com www.daviddavidgallery.com and www.askart.com/DDavid

Sarah Blum, most people can only imagine the atrocities you experiences. Thank you for sharing them. To contact Sarah and see her products go to http://womenunderfire.net.

Bill Seavey, Thank you for sending me your book Greener Pastures and sharing your story. You can learn more about Bill and his inspirational books and products by going to www.williamseavey.com

Frank Healy

About the Author

Frank Healy is a Licensed Professional Counselor in the State of New Jersey and Certified Life Coach. He is classified with Hyperthymesia or Highly Superior Autobiographical Memory by the University of California. Frank remembers every day of his life for the past 49 years since he was six years old. This includes the day of the week, the weather, news, and personal events. Frank lives with his wife Janet in Dennisville New Jersey and works as a therapist at AtlantiCare Behavioral Health and Associates For Life Enhancement. Frank's other books include Heal Your Memories, Change Your Life https://www.amazon.com/Heal-Your-Memories-Change-Life/dp/1452579679 https://www.amazon.com/Heal-Your-Memories-Change-Revised-ebook/dp/B00RRD7UJ2. Memory Brain Exercises https://www.amazon.com/Memory-Brain-Exercises-Increase-Strategies-ebook/dp/B01619W506 and Empower Yourself Through Your Memorieshttps://www.amazon.com/Empower-Yourself-Through-Your-Memories/dp/1546831460 https://www.amazon.com/Empower-Yourself-Through-Your-Memories-ebook/dp/B01N32B4E6

Frank has been a guest on the Michael Smerconish radio show. He has been a guest on True Life Academy and Be The Star You Are with Cynthia Brian. He has been on the CBS and NBC New Health Check. You can contact Frank at his website www.phenomenalmemory.com or email him at frank@phenomenalmemory.com

Resources

ABC News, Wednesday August 1, 2001, Action News,WPVI TV. Philadelphia, Pennsylvania

Aron, Elaine, **The Highly Sensitive Person, How to Thrive When the World Overwhelms You.** Harmony June 2, 1997. Harmony

Atlantic Cape Community College, Established November 19, 1964. Campuses in Mays Landing and Cape May Court House New Jersey.

Blum, Sarah, Personal Interview May 26, 2015

Byrne, Rhonda. **The Secret**, November 2006, Atria Books, Beyond Words Publishing, Hillsboro, Oregon

David, Carl, Personal Interview June 2, 2015

Rogers, David. **Get Which Quick,** A Play in 3 Acts,1966, Chicago, Dramatic Publishing.

Elston, Jennifer, Personal Communication

Ezine Articles, Chris Knight, SparkNET, www.Ezinearticles.com

Healy, Dolores, Personal communication

Healy, Frank Jr. Personal Communication

Healy, Mark, Personal Communication

Hisdates.com, Exploring the Past,www.hisdates.com

Issacson, Walter. **Steve Jobs,** 2011 Simon and Schuster, 2, New York, New York.

Learning Library, www.learninglibrary.com

London, Richard, Personal Interview, June 4, 2015

McElfresh, Angi, Personal Interview, July 12, 2015

Meister, Kelly, Personal Interview, May 26, 2015

Miller, Richard, Personal Communication

Press Of Atlantic City, The, Monday August 1, 2005.www.pressofatlanticcity.com

Seavey, Bill, Personal Interview, June 19, 2015

Robbins, Anthony. Personal Power II; The Driving Force. CD series. 1996 Guthy Renker, 41550 Eclectic St. # 200, Palm Desert, Ca. 92260.

Schulz, Charles, **You're A Winner Charlie Brown,** 1960, Fawcett Crest Books. Robbinsdale, Mnnesota.

Schwartz, Sherwood, creator, **The Brady Bunch**, 1969-1974, Producer Levi Schwartz Paramount Television

Seavey, Bill. Greener Pastures, Acronym Attic, Greener Pastures Institute

Tong, Dean, Personal Interview, June 2, 2015

Web MD. **EMDR** https://www.webmd.com/mental-health/emdr-what-is-it

Dolman, Bob, and Howard, Ron **Far and Away**, May 22,1992. Salmon, Mikael, Cinematographer. Williams, John,Music Producer. Imagine Films Entertainment,, Universal Pictures. Universal City, California.

Wikepedia,**NormanCousins**
en.wikipedia.org/wiki/NormanCousins